CAMBRIDGE
UNIVERSITY PRESS

Coding Club

Python Basics

level 1

Chris Roffey

CAMBRIDGE
UNIVERSITY PRESS

University Printing House, Cambridge CB2 8BS, United Kingdom

Cambridge University Press is part of the University of Cambridge.

It furthers the University's mission by disseminating knowledge in the pursuit of education, learning and research at the highest international levels of excellence.

www.cambridge.org
Information on this title: www.cambridge.org/9781107658554

First published 2012
3rd printing 2014

Printed in Poland by Opolgraf

A catalogue record for this publication is available from the British Library

ISBN 978-1-107-65855-4 Paperback

Contents

Introduction

Why was this book written?

This book is the first in a series of books for anyone with little or no knowledge of computer programming but who would like to give it a go.

Who is this book for?

One factor was the availability of a computer that any child could save up for or get for their birthday, such as the Raspberry Pi from www.raspberrypi.org.

But my wish to produce a series of short books on coding goes back much further than that. When I grew up, computers were very different from the PCs we use today. To play a game or use a word-processor, you had to run the program by typing green text into an empty black screen. But the great thing was, you could also type in your own commands and run them! It was not long before I had written my first text-based game in a language called BASIC.

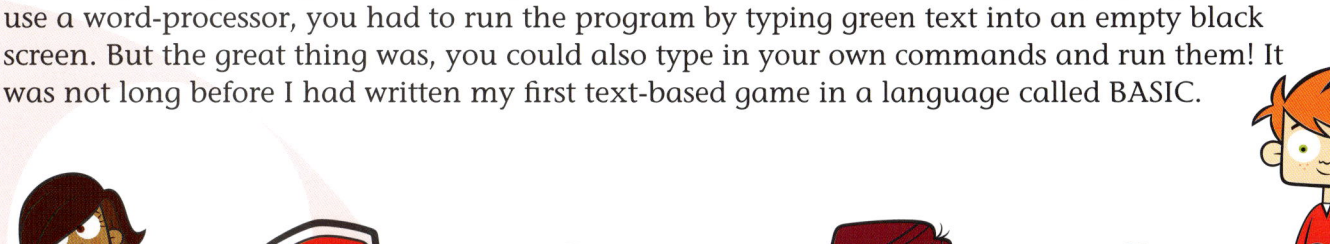

Later on, I wanted to learn a more modern language, and set about teaching myself Java. I read four or five books and completed the examples, but at the end of each one I was left in a dreadful situation: I had all sorts of ideas for programs I wished to make, but still no idea how to start! I could make the exciting projects that were the focus of these books, but not much else. So with this series of books, I have taken a different approach. I hope it will teach you the skills you need to write any program you can imagine – eventually – and many simple programs straight away.

Why should you choose this book?

After many years of looking, I finally found a great book on Java called *Introducing Java* by David Parsons, published by Thomas Learning. It was for university students. Suddenly I understood why we did certain things and how to start designing complex programs. If only I had started with this book to begin with!

I want you, the reader, to learn not only how to make the programs in this book but also how to design your own. I want you to be able to write programs well, so that if you take it further and become the inventor of the next Google you will not have to unlearn bad programming habits. Unlearning things, I should add, is a lot more difficult than you might imagine.

What needs to be installed?

You do not have to do this! Please ask a responsible adult to read the *Introduction for Adults* page on the coding club website (www.codingclub.co.uk) so that they can get everything organised for you. If you are able to do this by yourself then full instructions can be found at http://python.org/download/. If you are going to learn to program on a Raspberry Pi, it will be very easy to get things ready as it comes pre-installed with everything you need. You do not have to use a Raspberry Pi to run Python. You can use Windows, Apple Mac and Linux systems.

How to use this book

It is hoped that you will read this book carefully and build all the main projects in order. At the end of each chapter there are further ideas, and challenges that you can think of as 'mini quests' in a video game. Some readers will want to work through all of them so that they understand everything all the time. Some of you will probably prefer to rush through and get to the end. When these readers think: 'What can I do now?' One answer is to go back and look at some of the ideas at the end of each chapter. Which approach is best? The one you are most comfortable with. If you are being guided by a teacher though, then to enable them to help you the most you should trust their judgement.

There are four ways in which this book tries to help you to learn:

1 By copying the code – this is important as it gets you to work through the code a line at a time (like computers do) and will help you remember the details in the future.
2 Finding and fixing errors – error messages in Python give you some clues as to what has gone wrong. Solving these problems yourself will help you to be a better programmer. In the end though, this should not become boring, so if you get stuck the code can be downloaded from the accompanying website.
3 Experimenting – feel free to experiment with the code we write. See what else you can make it do. If you try all the challenges, puzzles and ideas, and generally mess with the code, this will help you learn how to write code like a professional.
4 Finally, this book will not only provide the code to build some cool, short projects but also teach you how the programs were designed. You can then use the same methods to design your own applications.

A word of warning

You may be tempted to simply get the code off the web site instead of typing it yourself. If you do this you will probably find that you cannot remember how to write code so easily later. You will only be asked to type small chunks of code at a time – remember that this will help you understand every detail of your programs.

You will also become a faster typist, which is a very important skill these days!

Chapter 1
Python, IDLE and your first program

In this chapter you are going to:

- learn about computer programming and the different languages that you can use

- meet the Python programming language

- learn how to use IDLE, which will help organise your programs and allow you to run them easily

- check that your computer has been set up correctly

- write and run your first program.

I am never IDLE, although I do occasionally get a bit sleepy...zzzz.

Coding

Coding is writing instructions for a computer to perform a task. This code has to be in a form that the computer can understand. This is more formally known as computer programming.

Computers and coding have not been around for a long time but they have sure packed in some interesting history in a short space of time. The first machine that stored instructions in a way that future computers could take advantage of was the Jacquard loom that used holes punched in cards and was invented in 1801. Charles Babbage is often credited with inventing the first computer which he described in 1837 but was not built until 100 years later. In 1989 Guido van Rossum started to create the Python programming language which he named after Monty Python's Flying Circus, a BBC comedy sketch show.

Programming languages

There are many programming languages currently used by coders around the world. Some are best in one situation, others in another.

- Fortran is excellent at high precision maths calculations.

- SQL is great at making databases do what you want.

- Python is brilliant for writing quick applications, running programming experiments and for building larger applications, including games.

If you have previously programmed in Scratch (produced by MIT) you will find you can pick up Python very quickly. Scratch is great for learning how to think like a programmer and is very good for making games. If you have not tried Scratch before, you might enjoy trying that next because the ability to learn a new programming language is an important skill for coders. You will find it is a lot easier than learning a new human language.

Once you have learned one modern programming language, you can quickly learn others. You simply have to find out how your new language handles variables, loops, etc. (You will know what these are by the end of the book.)

Python

Python is a typed computer language. This makes writing short programs very fast and you can produce almost anything you can imagine.

Python is a powerful, modern programming language used by many famous organisations such as YouTube and NASA. It is one of three programming languages that can be used to write Google Apps. Python is a great language. Enjoy!

IDLE

You will start programming in IDLE which comes with Python. IDLE is a special text editor like Microsoft Word, except it understands Python and helps you get your code right. IDLE is itself, a Python application.

Python is also one of the languages used by the European Particle Accelerator organisation, CERN.

Let's look at IDLE:

```
● ● ●                        Python Shell
Python 3.2.1 (v3.2.1:ac1f7e5c0510, Jul 9 2011, 01:03:53)
[GCC 4.2.1 (Apple Inc. build 5666) (dot 3)] on darwin
Type "copyright", "credits" or "license()" for more information.
>>>
                                                    Ln: 4 Col: 4
```

IDLE when started on an Apple Mac.

It is important when learning a programming language to learn the special vocabulary that goes with it. This is because when you want to try to find something out, you know which keywords to search for. This is why new 'computer speak' words appear in bold. This means that they will be explained in the glossary at the end of the book. Obviously bold will not appear in the glossary!

The code you want to run is typed after the special entry prompt:

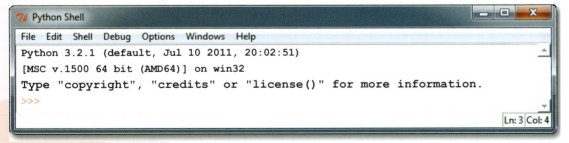

>>> my code goes here

To run the code we press the return key. This is how Python runs in IDLE's **interactive mode**. Python can run files as well but to start with, this is all we need.

Let's see how IDLE looks on a Windows PC:

```
7% Python Shell                                    □ ▣ X
 File  Edit  Shell  Debug  Options  Windows  Help
Python 3.2.1 (default, Jul 10 2011, 20:02:51)
[MSC v.1500 64 bit (AMD64)] on win32
Type "copyright", "credits" or "license()" for more information.
>>>
                                                    Ln: 3 Col: 4
```

IDLE when started on Windows 7.

And finally, how IDLE looks on a Linux computer:

IDLE when started up on the Raspberry Pi computer.

A great reason for learning Python and using IDLE as our **IDE** (Integrated Development Environment) is that it is very similar on all the different types of computers available.

The text before the >>> prompt is unimportant at the moment. However, it is always useful to know what version of Python you are using.

Hello World!

Since the dawn of programming, when the first cave-coders booted up their cave-computers, it has been a tradition that your first program when learning a new language is 'Hello World'. The aim is to try to make the computer say 'hello' to the world. If you can do this you will have tested whether everything that was set up for you is working properly.

- If it is not already started, start up IDLE.

- After the >>> prompt write in the code from Code Box 1.1 and then press your return key to run the program.

Code Box 1.1
```
print("Hello World!")
```

If all is well, you should get something like this:

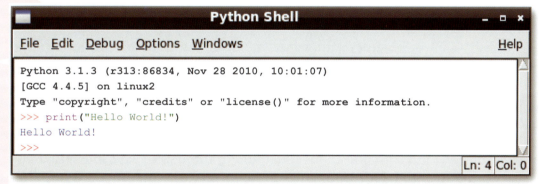

```
Python Shell                                    _ ▫ ✕

File  Edit  Debug  Options  Windows                    Help

Python 3.1.3 (r313:86834, Nov 28 2010, 10:01:07)
[GCC 4.4.5] on linux2
Type "copyright", "credits" or "license()" for more information.
>>> print("Hello World!")
Hello World!
>>>

                                             Ln: 4 Col: 0
```

Hello World!

Python has followed your instruction and **output** 'Hello World!'

You have written your first computer program. Well done!

This might not seem much to you, but you have given your computer a direct instruction that you have written yourself and it has carried out your instruction. From this small seed, great applications will grow!

Making mistakes

Did you get a syntax error?

Syntax errors are very common when typing in code (as are other errors). If you make one or two it is not your fault. It is because although computers are fast, they can also be a bit stupid. If there are any tiny mistakes in your code, they panic and produce error messages. These messages try to explain to you what the problem is but they are often difficult to understand.

Colons, brackets, speech marks, apostrophes and spelling of Python words have to be just right. Although we can read imperfect sentences, computers cannot.

Whether or not you got any errors, try this Quick Quiz.

Quick Quiz 1

Which of these lines of code are correct?
```
1 Print("Hello world!")
2 print("Hello world!")
3 print(Hello world!)
4 print "Hello world!"
```

I do not make errors.

Am I a syntax error?

Notice how the coloured text helps you spot code that is not going to work. All the code listings in this book use the same coloured text as in IDLE's standard display. This should help you to spot **bugs** in your code.

Chapter summary

In this chapter you have learned:

- that programming is writing instructions for computers
- that there are many different computer languages
- why Python is a great language to learn
- how to use IDLE in interactive mode
- how to write and run a simple program
- that the `print()` command means 'show on the screen' not 'send to the printer'.

Idea 1

1 Write some new code so that a short message is displayed that says thank you to whoever got everything ready for you.
2 Run your new code to display the message.
3 Now show them your message. This will make them happy.

Idea 2

1 Write some code so that the computer will show the text for a joke.
```
>>> print("Question: What goes clip?")
Question: What goes clip?
>>> print("Answer: A one legged horse")
Answer: A one legged horse
>>>
```

This is one of my favourite jokes!

Chapter 2
Some text, some maths and going loopy

In this chapter you are going to:

- learn how to do some more with text

- get Python to do some maths for you

- learn about how `while` loops work

- learn lots of useful operators.

This is a fun chapter as we get to start some real programming!

Going loopy? I've got that covered!

Text

Escape sequences

Try opening IDLE in interactive mode and enter the code in Code Box 2.1.

Code Box 2.1   x

```
print("Question: What goes clip?\nAnswer: A one legged horse.")
```

If you have not pressed your return key yet, to see what happens, do so now.

You should have discovered \n has a special purpose. It is an example of an **escape sequence**. Table 2.1 shows some more escape sequences.

Escape sequence	What it does
\n	creates a line return in a string of text
\t	creates a tab style indent in a string of text
\\	allows a backslash to appear in a string of text
\"	allows a speech mark to be used in a string of text

Table 2.1 Escape sequences.

Experiment

Try writing a variety of little programs in IDLE using the escape sequences in Table 2.1 until you feel you know what they all do.

Backslashes

Are you a bit confused about the last two escape sequences? If so, type in and run the code from Code Box 2.2.

Code Box 2.2

```
print("Here is a speech mark: \" and here is a slash: \\")
```

Try typing in the code from Code Box 2.3 to see how to avoid having to escape speech marks. This takes advantage of the fact that you can choose whether to surround strings in double speech marks or single ones. Watch out though, you will get a lot of syntax errors if you do not do this carefully.

Code Box 2.3

```
print('I say "High", you say "Low". You say "Why?" and I say "I don\'t know". Oh no.')
```

The backslash is used to 'escape' characters that are used in Python. When we want to print some text to the screen we wrap it in speech marks. This now means that there is a problem if you want to type some speech marks. Well, you know what to do about it – put a backslash before it. So what do you do if you want to actually print a backslash to the screen? Put a backslash before it!

Did you know that us Coders call text, strings?

Functions

`print()` is called a **function** (these are covered in chapter 4, page 53). What `print()` will do, is print anything you throw at it inside the brackets. They must be separated by a comma, and **strings** (bits of text) must be put in speech marks. Everything inside the brackets will be printed out in order. The results from sums can also be output, but you must not put the calculations in speech marks. What do you think would happen if you left in the speech marks? Don't forget you can also add in escape sequences.

Maths

Using Python as a calculator is easy, if you remember two things:

1 In Python, as in almost all programming languages, the multiplication symbol is an asterisk.
2 The division symbol is a forward slash.

```
>>> 10/4
2.5
>>> 3*3
9
>>>
```

There is another way of dividing. If you use two forward slashes instead of one, Python will produce an **integer** as an answer. An integer is a whole number (a decimal such as 2.5 is called a **float**). You can now find the remainder, with another **mathematical operator** called the **modulus**. This is represented by a % sign.

```
>>> 11/4
2.75
>>> 11//4
2
>>> 11%4
3
>>>
```

Table 2.2 lists some more mathematical operators.

Operator	Name	Example	Answer
*	multiply	2*3	6
/	divide (normal)	20/8	2.5
//	divide (integer)	20//8	2
%	modulus	20%8	4
+	add	2+3	5
−	subtract	7−3	4

Table 2.2 Maths operators.

Ooh maths!

Ooh strings!

Experiment

In interactive mode, check that the examples in Table 2.2 do give the correct answers and then try out some of your own favourite sums. You might like to see what happens if you wrap a maths sum inside speech marks in the `print()` function.

Combining text and maths

It is also possible to combine text (or strings) and numbers in the `print()` function. The comma is used here as a separator between the text and the maths.

```
>>> print("111 divided by 4 = ", 111/4)
111 divided by 4 = 27.75
>>>
>>> print("11 divided by 4 = ", 11/4)
11 divided by 4 = 2.75
>>>
```

? Quick Quiz 2

Can you work out what the output from this code will be?

```
>>> print("11 divided by 4 also equals: ", 11//4, " remainder: ", 11%4)
```

Going loopy

Computers are great at repetitive tasks. So are humans, but we get bored easily! Computers are not only good at them, they are fast! Therefore we need to know how to tell them to do repeats. To do this we use a **while loop**. This runs some code while something is true and stops when it becomes false.

Imagine you were trying to write some code in a History lesson at school, when you should be doing History. Your teacher might ask you to write fifty lines. Well no matter, Python can do that.

Try opening IDLE in interactive mode and then enter the code in Code Box 2.4. You will need to press return twice at the end.

Wow! Python can multiply strings as well.

Code Box 2.4

```
>>> lines=0
>>> while lines < 50:
        print("I will not write code in history lessons.")
        lines = lines+1
```

Here is another solution to the same problem:

Code Box 2.5

```
>>> print("I will not write code in history lessons.\n" *50)
```

The code in Code Box 2.5 is clever – look carefully to see what is happening. Run it if you are not sure. Although the code in Code Box 2.4 is longer, a while loop is often more useful as it can do far more complex tasks. For example, with a while loop you can ask a computer to count to 100. Try entering the code from Code Box 2.6 and running it.

Code Box 2.6

```
>>> number=1
>>> while number < 101:
        print(number)
        number = number+1
```

How do while loops work?

Variables

To start with we create a **variable** and assign a value to it. A variable is a space in the computer's memory where we can store, for example, a string or an integer. We create a variable by naming it. In Code Box 2.6 we called our variable 'number' and with the **equals operator** we give it the value '1'.

The next line of code >>> while number<101: says 'while the variable called number is less than 101 do the following'. All of the code that is indented after the colon is to be repeatedly performed by the computer. That is, it loops through these two lines of code until number is no longer less than 101.

create a variable and assign it the value 1

```
number=1
while number < 1:
    print(number)
    number = number+1
```

the colon says to run all of the indented code

there are no speech marks here as we want the value of number not the word "number"

the variable number is incremented by 1

IDLE automatically indents for you!

The last line of code number = number+1 is in the loop. It keeps adding 1 to number for each passage through the loop. Don't forget the variable's value can be changed with the equals operator at any time.

Delving Deeper

The equals sign is used differently to the way it is used in maths. In computing, the equals sign means 'point this variable name at this piece of data' (an integer for example). So number=1 means 'create a variable called number and point it at the integer 1'. Another way of saying this is 'assign the value 1 to the variable number'. Later we may assign another value to number.

I like to think of number = 1 as meaning: 'make the variable called number equal to 1, for now...'

Operators

There are several operators you can use in a while loop. Some examples are given in Table 2.3. Note how we now have another version of equals ==. This form is more like the equals in maths. It is an example of a **comparative operator**. Therefore, `while` `number==1:` means 'while the variable called `number` is equal to 1, do the following'.

Operator	Meaning
==	equal to
!=	not equal to
>	greater than
<	less than
>=	greater than or equal to
<=	less than or equal to

Table 2.3 Comparative operators.

We use a double equals sign to compare two values and a single equals sign to assign a value to a variable.

My father works for a bus operator in London.

Chapter summary

In this chapter you have learned:

- how the `print()` function is very flexible
- how to write and run simple maths code
- how to output a mixture of strings, maths or numbers
- how to write a while loop and use comparative operators

Puzzle 1

Write some code in IDLE so that the computer counts up to 20 in twos.

Puzzle 2

Write some code so that the computer outputs the 5 times table like this.

```
1x5=5
2x5=10
3x5=15
```

Hint: You will need a counter variable which you could call `number`. Then you should find out how to write one line, and then make your loop do it 10 times.

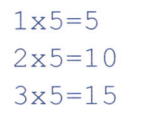

I love puzzles!

Puzzle 3

See if you can re-write the following code in three different ways so that each program still produces output which counts to a hundred.

```
>>> number=1
>>> while number < 101:
        print(number)
        number = number+1
```

In your new code, you are not allowed to use the less than operator <. Instead you should use one of these comparative operators in each program:
<= > !=

If you write some code that will not stop running, just close the IDLE window. When you are asked if you want to kill the program, click the OK button. Unfortunately, you will have to start up IDLE again.

Answers to all of these puzzles can be found on the companion website www.codingclub.co.uk.

Chapter 3
Readable code and the MyMagic8Ball game

In this chapter you are going to:

- write and save a Python file using script mode

- learn how to write clear readable code

- run a Python file

- learn about how to get user input

- learn about `if` and `else`

- write a short game called MyMagic8Ball.

You are going to build and save a Magic 8 Ball game. If you have not played with one of these toys before, what you do is, ask the 8 Ball for some advice, shake it and it magically responds.

Magic 8 Ball, are you really magic?

I might be...

Script mode

Open IDLE in interactive mode and then from the *File* menu choose *New Window*. A new window appears that is apparently blank. When you type in this window and save the file you are working in **script mode**. The file name must end in `.py` to show that it is Python code.

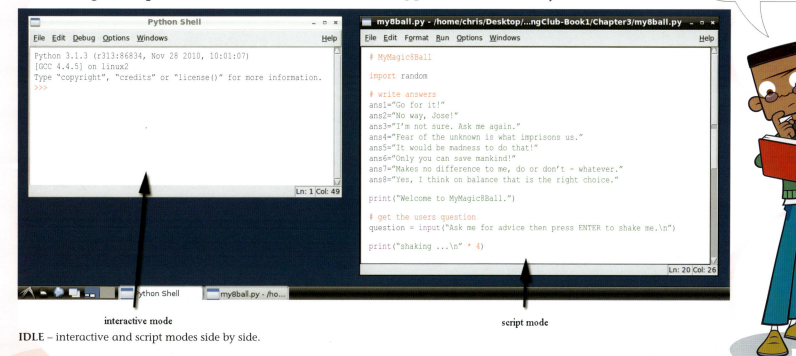

```
Python Shell                                    _ □ ×

File  Edit  Debug  Options  Windows                        Help

Python 3.1.3 (r313:86834, Nov 28 2010, 10:01:07)
[GCC 4.4.5] on linux2
Type "copyright", "credits" or "license()" for more information.
>>>




                                                    Ln: 1 Col: 49
```

```
my8ball.py - /home/chris/Desktop/...ngClub-Book1/Chapter3/my8ball.py    _ □ ×

File  Edit  Format  Run  Options  Windows                        Help

# MyMagic8Ball

import random

# write answers
ans1="Go for it!"
ans2="No way, Jose!"
ans3="I'm not sure. Ask me again."
ans4="Fear of the unknown is what imprisons us."
ans5="It would be madness to do that!"
ans6="Only you can save mankind!"
ans7="Makes no difference to me, do or don't - whatever."
ans8="Yes, I think on balance that is the right choice."

print("Welcome to MyMagic8Ball.")

# get the users question
question = input("Ask me for advice then press ENTER to shake me.\n")

print("shaking ...\n" * 4)

                                                    Ln: 20 Col: 26
```

interactive mode   script mode

IDLE – interactive and script modes side by side.

Try typing the code from Code Box 3.1 into your new script mode window. These are the first lines of the MyMagic8Ball game.

(If you have a British Apple keyboard, you will need to hold *alt* and click the £ symbol to type #.)

Code Box 3.1

```
# MyMagic8Ball

import random

# write answers
ans1="Go for it!"
ans2="No way, Jose!"
ans3="I'm not sure. Ask me again."
ans4="Fear of the unknown is what imprisons us."
ans5="It would be madness to do that!"
ans6="Only you can save mankind!"
ans7="Makes no difference to me, do or don't - whatever."
ans8="Yes, I think on balance that is the right choice."
```

Now you should save your work by choosing *Save* from the *File* menu. It is a good idea to save all your code into a special folder which you can call – 'Python Code' – in your *documents* folder. Call the new file myMagic8Ball.py.

Analysis of Code Box 3.1

The # symbol

The # symbol says to the computer, 'ignore the rest of the text on this line, it is for humans'. This is called **commenting**. You have typed in two comments so far.

Me llamo José.

Modules

`import random` uses a new Python word – `import` – followed by the name of a Python module.

A module is a Python file with special code that you do not have to write yourself but that you can use. There are many modules available and it is also possible to write your own. So `import random` brings in to your application a selection of **functions** that you can use later in your program. (Chapter 4 is all about functions.)

String variables

The last 8 lines of code are the variables where you store some strings (bits of text) that will be used later in the game. At this early stage you may be asking yourself, how do I know what to call my variables? Well within reason you can call them what you like. There are only 31 reserved words in Python.

Writing tidy code

It is important to write your code so that it is easy for you to read it later, when you have forgotten how you did things. It also makes it easier, if your code is well written, for other coders to understand what you did.

White space

Lots of computer languages like Java, PHP and C++ wrap chunks of code in curly brackets. Each statement has to end in a semicolon.

Delving Deeper

There are 31 Python words that you cannot use as your own variable names. These are:
```
and as assert break class continue
def del elif else except finally
for from global if import in is
lambda nonlocal not or pass print
raise return try while with yield
```

You must also be very careful to use only letters and underscores and no unusual characters such as & ! @ $ * ( ) ? : ; [ ] " < > ' ` | = { } \ /. Spaces are not allowed either. Numbers are allowed but not at the beginning of your variable names.

```
{
    private int current_floor = 0;
    public int getFloor()
    {
        return current_floor;
    }
    public void moveToFloor(int floor_number)
    {
        current_floor = floor_number;
    }
}
```

Java code.

Python does not require semicolons or curly brackets. Semicolons can be very annoying as they are easy to forget and if you do forget one, your program will not run at all.

In Python, each line of code simply requires that you have a line ending. This is a lot easier to spot if you do manage to forget!

To group lines of code together you indent the code (four taps on the space bar). However IDLE will usually know when you should indent and do it for you when you press return! This indenting produces 'white space'. The code is grouped according to how you arrange the white space. This is how the same code would look in Python.

```
class Lift():
    current_floor=0

    def getFloor():
        return current_floor

    def moveToFloor(floor_number):
        current_floor = floor_number
```

Python code.

Remember though that incorrect indenting in Python, such as 3 spaces instead of 4, will cause errors.

I prefer the look of Python code.

More about commenting

Don't be surprised if you had no idea what any of the code above meant. Even if you had already read this book, it can be difficult to read other people's code. Remember, it is written for computers to understand, not us. Remember, we can leave little notes or comments as we go using the hash symbol #.

Here is the same Python code as above with some comments.

```python
# This is a class that describes a lift (or elevator in the USA)
class Lift():
    # The lift starts on floor zero
    current_floor=0

    # The method for finding the lift
    def getFloor():
        return current_floor

    # The method for moving the lift
    def moveToFloor(floor_number):
        current_floor = floor_number
```

Python code with too many comments.

As you can see, it is possible to add too much commenting! Sometimes simply naming things well is much better. The names chosen by the programmer here include `Lift`, `current_floor`, `getFloor`, `moveToFloor` and `floor_number`. The only Python code words are `class` and `def`.

Naming variables

If you want to store a number or some text somewhere you do so in a variable.

Variables should always be named with descriptive names. You should always start with a little letter. You can separate words with underscores like this `my_own_variable`.

Getting user input

Getting user input is surprisingly simple in Python. We use another supplied function `input()`. This function is very similar to the `print()` function in as much as it can be given a string which it sends to the screen. The difference is it can only take one string and it then waits for the return key on the keyboard to be pressed. This means that it can be used to pause a program or wait until the user is ready. However it does one other thing: it returns, as a string, everything that is typed by the user until the return key is pressed. This can be collected in a string variable like this.

```
keyboard_input = input("Enter some text please.")
```

Python does not require that you name variables like this but if you want the respect of other coders you will!

Experiment

- In interactive mode, try typing the code in Code Box 3.2 to see how this works. When the computer asks for your name, tell it who you are, press return and then complete the code.

Code Box 3.2

```
>>> name = input("What is your name?\n")
>>> print("Hello ", name)
```

- Try and see what you can do with `input()` without supplying any text.

- By combining `print()` with `input()` you can make up for input's inability to handle complicated combinations of strings and maths. See if you can work out how. (Hint: Just use `input()` on its own, after a complicated `print()` function.)

Now back to script mode.

After your eight variables in `myMagic8Ball.py`, miss a line and type in the code from Code Box 3.3.

Code Box 3.3

```
print("Welcome to MyMagic8Ball.")
# get the users question
question = input("Ask me for advice then press RETURN to shake me.\n")
print("shaking ...\n" * 4)
```

The variable `question` is given the value from the result of the `input()` function. That is, it now stores whatever was typed by the person playing the game before they pressed return. In this version you will not use this variable. In fact the player might as well speak. However, you may want to customise the game later so it is good design to store this input somewhere obvious, just in case. You will find that you understand the rest of this code now. If you are not sure what the last line in Code Box 3.3 does, you could copy that into the interactive mode window and find out.

Using the random module

The first line of code in Code Box 3.1 imports Python's random module. This gives your program access to a number of functions. You will use just one – `randint()`. This function takes two integer **arguments**. Arguments are the values that you provide for a function to do its task. You will learn more about this in chapter 4.

A simple dice

To create a dice requires only one line of code in interactive mode.

```
>>> random.randint(1, 6)
```

We have to put `random.` before `randint()` to tell the computer that this function can be found in the random module. The two arguments are the start number and the end number. The function randomly chooses 1, 2, 3, 4, 5 or 6. Try it out a few times in interactive mode to see it in action.

I may be a simple dice but I am a very complex individual.

Back in script mode

Back in the `myMagic8Ball.py` window type the code from Code Box 3.4. You will see that we use the `randint()` function to generate a random number between 1 and 8 and assign the result to a variable called `choice`.

(**Hint**: You can save yourself a lot of typing by copying and pasting. Remember that whenever you do this, it means there is probably a better way of writing your code!)

I would have thought that the best way of doing this would be with tuples.

Well probably yes, but our readers will not meet tuples in this book.

Code Box 3.4

```python
# use the randint() function to select the correct answer
choice=random.randint(1, 8)
if choice == 1:
    answer=ans1
elif choice == 2:
    answer=ans2
elif choice == 3:
    answer=ans3
elif choice == 4:
    answer=ans4
elif choice == 5:
    answer=ans5
elif choice == 6:
    answer=ans6
elif choice == 7:
    answer=ans7
```

A random image!

(continues on the next page)

```
else:
    answer=ans8

# print the answer to the screen
print(answer)

input("\n\nPress the RETURN key to finish.")
```

Analysis of Code Box 3.4

if, elif and else

The last part of the code in Code Box 3.4 used the Python words `if`, `elif` and `else`. They are very easy to understand when you realise that `elif` is short for else if. Look at this bit of code.

```
if choice == 1:
    answer = ans1
```

The first line says, 'if the value of `choice` is equal to 1, then run the code that is indented after the colon.'

Notice how the comparison operator `==` is used, in the same way as it was with the while loop in chapter 2.

So, if `choice` does equal 1 the program creates a new variable and calls it `answer`. Using the equals sign it is given the string that is held by your variable `ans1` which you typed at the beginning of the program. So now `answer` would hold the string `"Go for it!"`.

The random generator `randint(1, 8)` may not have produced the value 1 though, so the next bit of the code handles the situation if `choice` equals `2:`.

```
elif choice == 2:
    answer=ans2
```

So in this case `answer` would hold the string, `"No way, Jose!"`.

This continues until the application handles all other situations with `else:`.
In your program this means if the choice is 8.

```
else:
    answer=ans8
```

Two uses of input

The `input()` function is used twice in this program. The first time, it takes the user input and stores it in a variable called `question`.

It is perfectly OK to have just an **if** statement on its own. It is also OK to simply have an **if** statement followed by **else**. If you use an **elif** statement though, you must end with **else**.

```
question = input("Ask me for advice then press ENTER to shake me.\n")
```

Do you remember how the user's input is not actually required? What this line of code does do, is wait until the return key is pressed and stores the input just in case we decide to use it some other time.

At the end of the program we use the `input()` function again.

```
input("\n\nPress the RETURN key to finish.")
```

This line does not even bother storing the user input at all. It just supplies two line returns and a message to say the game is over. The program again waits for the user to press the return key and then finishes.

This is much better than suddenly finishing the game unexpectedly and you will see it used a lot from now on.

You have entered all the code for this program now. If you have not saved it, do so now and then check it against the complete listing in Code Box 3.5.

Putting it all together

Here is the complete code as seen in IDLE.

Code Box 3.5

```
# MyMagic8Ball

import random

# write answers
ans1="Go for it!"
ans2="No way, Jose!"
ans3="I'm not sure. Ask me again."
ans4="Fear of the unknown is what imprisons us."
ans5="It would be madness to do that!"
ans6="Only you can save mankind!"
ans7="Makes no difference to me, do or don't - whatever."
ans8="Yes, I think on balance that is the right choice."

print("Welcome to MyMagic8Ball.")

# get the users question
question = input("Ask me for advice then press ENTER to shake me.\n")

print("shaking ...\n" * 4)
# use the randint() function to select the correct answer
choice=random.randint(1, 8)
if choice==1:
    answer=ans1
```

(continues on the next page)

```python
elif choice==2:
    answer=ans2
elif choice==3:
    answer=ans3
elif choice==4:
    answer=ans4
elif choice==5:
    answer=ans5
elif choice==6:
    answer=ans6
elif choice==7:
    answer=ans7
else:
    answer=ans8

# print the answer to the screen
print(answer)

input("\n\nPress the RETURN key to finish.")
```

Running programs in script mode

To run the code you must first remember to save it with the `.py` at the end. Now with the finished `myMagic8Ball.py` file open, choose *Run Module* from the *Run* menu. The program will run in the interactive mode window. Try it out.

Chapter summary

In this chapter you have learned:

- how to write and save a Python file using script mode
- how to write clear readable code with comments and descriptive variable names
- how to run a Python file
- how to get user input
- about `if`, `elif` and `else`
- how to write a short game called MyMagic8Ball.

You have worked hard and learned a lot in this chapter. It is time you experimented a bit!

Fun! Fun! Fun!

Idea 1

Try out the game on some friends or relatives. (**Hint:** Make sure they cannot see the code, as this will ruin the game.)

Idea 2

Change the eight string variables to answers you want your Magic8Ball to say.

- Add some code to `myMagic8Ball.py` so that the Magic8Ball says 'Hi' and asks for the user's name at the start of the game.
- It should then store the input in a variable such as `user_name`.
- Re-write the code so that the Magic8Ball talks to the user using their name. At the end for example, it could say: 'Thanks for playing [user's name]. Please press the return key to finish.'

There are several ways to do this. An example answer can be found on the Coding Club website.

Chapter 4
Functions

In this chapter you are going to:

- learn about functions

- write your own functions

- create a number guessing game.

Guessing games can be cool.

Functions

You have already met and used a few functions. The first one you used was `print()`. Functions have brackets after their name. This is where we supply arguments separated by commas. Some functions do not need them, they do their jobs without argument!

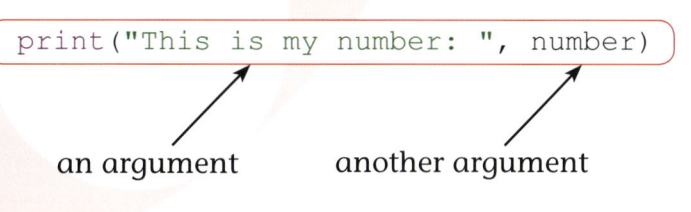

```
print("This is my number: ", number)
```

an argument   another argument

When we create or use a function that does not require any arguments, we still put empty brackets after its name.
e.g. `my_function()`

There are many functions that are built in to Python that we can already use. We can also make our own. We create functions with the `def` keyword. Here is the code for a counting function.

```
>>> def count(number):
        n=1
        while n <= number:
            print(n)
            n = n+1
```

In interactive mode, type in the above code. You will need to press return twice to get back to the Python prompt. Then type `count(10)` and press return.

An infinite loop ...
oh no!

```
1 × 12 = 12
2 × 12 = 24
3 × 12 = 36
4 × 12 = 48
5 × 12 = 60
6 × 12 = 72
```

Times tables anyone?

To get Python to produce any of the times tables is easy, with a `while` loop. However, if we want to be able to quickly choose which times table we want, then it is probably easier to write a new function rather than keep **hacking** your code.

Let's start thinking...

We need to supply a value that indicates which times table we want. This is a number so we could call this argument `num`:

```
def times_tables(num):
```

Now we need to produce a `while` loop. But first let's work out the code for one line of the table e.g. `2 × 12 = 24`. To do this the `2` is a counter which we will use in the while loop (Simply use `n`, not all variable names have to be descriptive!). The `12` is `num` and the `24` is obtained by multiplying n by num. The rest is just text. We can put all this together into one print **statement**.

? Quick Quiz 3

Which of these produces the output we want?

```
1 print(n, " x ", num, " = ", n*num)
2 print(num, " x ", n, " = ", num*n)
3 print(n, " * ", num, " = " n*num)
```

Now let's stick it all together.

Using IDLE's interactive mode, type in and think about the code in Code Box 4.1. Don't forget to press return twice to get back the Python prompt. Nothing should happen yet – all will be revealed shortly.

Code Box 4.1

```
>>> def times_tables(num):
        n=1
        while n <= 10:
            print(n, " x ", num, " = ", n*num)
            n = n+1
```

To run this code and output the 12 times table, type the code from Code Box 4.2 and press return.

Code Box 4.2 x

```
>>> times_tables(12)
```

If all goes well you should have a screen that looks like this:

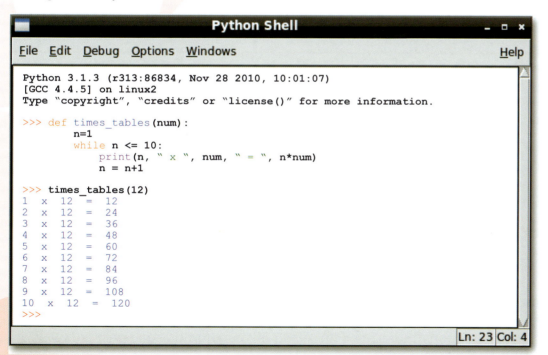

```
Python Shell                                    _ □ ✕

File  Edit  Debug  Options  Windows                Help

Python 3.1.3 (r313:86834, Nov 28 2010, 10:01:07)
[GCC 4.4.5] on linux2
Type "copyright", "credits" or "license()" for more information.

>>> def times_tables(num):
        n=1
        while n <= 10:
            print(n, " x ", num, " = ", n*num)
            n = n+1

>>> times_tables(12)
1   x   12   =   12
2   x   12   =   24
3   x   12   =   36
4   x   12   =   48
5   x   12   =   60
6   x   12   =   72
7   x   12   =   84
8   x   12   =   96
9   x   12   =   108
10  x   12   =   120
>>>
                                           Ln: 23 Col: 4
```

Times tables.

I prefer the googolplex times table.

My favourite times table is the 256 times table.

What if you prefer to have your times tables twelve lines long, so that you get 12 x 12 = 144. Now you have to go back and edit the function. This could become tiring in interactive mode and a small annoyance if your function was saved as a Python file. Let's try re-writing the function so that it takes two arguments instead. Still in interactive mode, try entering the code in Code Box 4.3 and you will see the power of functions. Enjoy!

If you still have the `times_tables():` function listed in your interactive mode window, try placing the cursor somewhere in `times_tables(num):` and then press return. This will copy the whole function and allow you to edit it. This trick can really speed up your typing. It works in script mode too.

Code Box 4.3

```
>>> def times_tables(how_far, num):
        n=1
        while n <= how_far:
            print(n, " x ", num, " = ", n*num)
            n = n+1
>>> times_tables(12, 17)
```

The number guessing game

Here is the complete code for a small game. This is a very simple game where the computer thinks of a number between 1 and 100 and the player has to guess what it is. The game uses Python's `random` number function again and a `while` loop. Open a new window in IDLE and type in the code from Code Box 4.4. Save this file as `myNumber.py` in your Python code folder. As you type, try and work out what each line is doing and marvel at how far you have come.

```python
# myNumber.py
# This game uses a home made function
import random

# Think of a number
computer_number = random.randint(1, 100)

# Create the function is_same()
def is_same(target, number):
    if target == number:
        result="Win"
    elif target > number:
        result="Low"
    else:
        result="High"
    return result

# Start the game
print("Hello.\nI have thought of a number between 1 and 100.")

# Collect the user's guess as an integer
guess = int(input("Can you guess it? "))
# Use our function
higher_or_lower = is_same(computer_number, guess)
```

(continues on the next page)

```python
# Run the game until the user is correct
while higher_or_lower != "Win":
    if higher_or_lower == "Low":
        guess = int(input("Sorry, you are too low. Try again. "))
    else:
        guess = int(input("Sorry, you are too high. Try again. "))

    higher_or_lower = is_same(computer_number, guess)

# End the game
input("Correct!\nWell Done\n\n\nPress RETURN to exit.")
```

There are two new things to you in this game. The `return` keyword tells the `is_same()` function what value should be sent back after it is called. We know functions can be sent arguments, well they can also return data.

In this case it returns the value stored in the variable `result`. So, if the two numbers are the same it returns the string `Win`, if the supplied number is higher than the target, the function returns the value `High` and if the supplied number is lower than the target, `Low`.

The second new thing to you is converting the user's input into an integer by wrapping it in `int( input goes here )`. This is because anything coming from keyboard input is received as strings. The process of converting one **data-type** into another data-type is called **casting**.

Have you remembered to save the file to your *Python Code* folder? If so, you can run it by choosing *Run Module* from the *Run* menu or pressing *F5*.

Chapter summary

In this chapter you have learned:

- about functions and how to write your own
- about building small programs, using functions and `while` loops
- a little about the steps needed when designing a function
- how to create a number guessing game
- how to stop a program that just keeps running – kill it; (or press *ctrl-c*)
- how to easily copy portions of code in IDLE.

You have worked hard and learned a lot about functions in this chapter. Here are a few ideas that you may enjoy. There are several ways to do them. Examples can be found on the web site.

Seriously, you can never have too much fun!

Idea 1

- Put the code from Code Box 4.3 into a script mode file called `times_tables.py`.
- Add some user interaction so that it asks which table you want and how far it should go.
- Do not forget to add a line of code to stop the program nicely.

Now you have a times table app you can use whenever you want.

Idea 2

Make a copy of `myNumber.py` and then add some code to make it count and display how many guesses it took the player. (**Hint:** you will need another variable which you could call `counter`.)

Idea 3

Make the `myNumber.py` game easier for younger children by reducing the range of numbers between 1 and 100 to between 1 and 10.

Idea 4

A harder challenge is to get the `myNumber.py` game to offer a choice of levels.
- Easy: choose from numbers between 1 and 10.
- Medium: numbers up to 20.
- Hard: numbers between 1 and 100.

This can be split into a number of shorter tasks.
1 Ask the user what level they would like to play and collect and store the new input as "e", "m" or "h".
2 Add the following code to catch any input we do not want the user to enter.

```
while level != "e" and level != "m" and level != "h":
    level = input("Sorry. You must type in one of the
                    letters 'e', 'm' or 'h'\ne/m/h:")
```

3 Use `if`, `elif` and `else` to sort out the upper limit and store the result in a suitable variable.
4 Move the code where the computer thinks of a number, to below this section and insert your upper limit variable in place of the appropriate argument.
5 Adjust the `print()` function below the `# Start the game` comment so that it outputs the correct information.
6 Adjust the code so the output all looks nice.

Chapter 5
MyEtchASketch

In this chapter you are going to:

- learn how to use the tkinter library

- make your own MyEtchASketch game

- learn how to put an application in its own window

- learn how to attach functions to keyboard presses.

The tkinter library

In the previous chapters we saw how to import a module. A module is a file that gives us access to a number of functions we do not have to write ourselves. So far we have used the random module.

We are now going to import a whole library of modules that give us access to graphical functions, such as the ability to make a window and a canvas to draw on.

As there are a number of modules we simply import them all like this.

```
from tkinter import *
```

The asterisk means everything. It is not being used as a multiplication symbol here!

As **tkinter** uses classes (which we are not learning about in this book), some of the code looks a bit strange. Do not worry about it. This is an introductory book. You can learn about classes later. The term `Canvas()` for example takes its arguments in a different form because `Canvas` is a class. Also notice it starts with a capital letter.

We are going to make a window that is 600 pixels (dots on the screen) wide and 400 pixels high with a canvas we can draw on. In our case the canvas is black. We do this using the code from Code Box 5.1. First we must open a new file in script mode and type it in.

Then save it as `myEtchASketch.py`

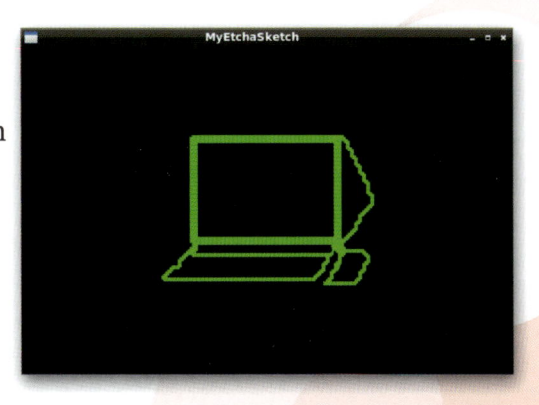

MyEtchASketch in a window.

Code Box 5.1

```python
# myEtchASketch application from Coding Club: Python Basics

from tkinter import *

##### Set variables:
canvas_height = 400
canvas_width = 600
canvas_colour = "black"

##### main:
window = Tk()
window.title("MyEtchASketch")
canvas = Canvas(bg=canvas_colour, height=canvas_height, width=canvas_width, highlightthickness=0)
canvas.pack()

window.mainloop()
```

You can try running `myEtchASketch.py` now. Although it is not very exciting, it is the first time you have made a window! Notice how something also happens in the interactive mode window. This is now acting as a console where we will get, among other things, error messages.

The plan

Now that you have a window in which to make your application and a canvas to draw on, it is time to start planning the rest of the application. To do this we break down the task into functions. First we need to be able to draw a vertical line a bit at a time and then horizontally. As these are going to be controlled by the up, down, left and right arrow keys on the keyboard it makes sense to have four functions that are all going to be similar and then attach those functions to the keys. So to start with, let's just try and create a function that draws a line up when we press the up key. If we can achieve this we know that we will be able to complete this project.

The coordinates

Unlike in maths, tkinter and most computer languages use coordinates that count from the top left of the screen. So our canvas looks like this.

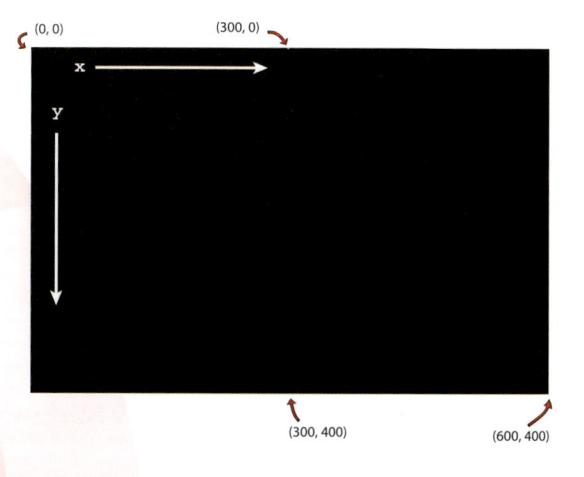

So a point on the screen is represented by two numbers:

e.g. (100, 50) = a point 100 pixels along the *x*-axis and 50 pixels down the *y*-axis.

Keeping code organised

The function to draw a vertical line requires a few more variables so that we can keep track of where we are up to. These should go at the top of your code with your other variable declarations. This is good coding style. Now if you want to adjust your program, you simply adjust the variables at the top and re-run it. You do not have to dig through your code to find where things happen. Also by choosing descriptive names for the variables you do not need excessive amounts of commenting.

The functions should come next. They need to be before the main section that runs your application. That way it can use them! Therefore the code from Code Box 5.1 has been split in Code Box 5.2 to make room for all our functions.

You can add the new code to your `myEtchASketch.py` file now. It will not do anything different yet. How the function works will be explained in the next analysis section.

```python
# myEtchASketch application from Coding Club: Python Basics

from tkinter import *

##### Set variables:
canvas_height = 400
canvas_width = 600
canvas_colour = "black"

p1_x = canvas_width/2
p1_y = canvas_height
p1_colour = "green"
line_width = 5
line_length = 5

##### Functions:

# player controls
def p1_move_N(event):
    global p1_y
```

```
canvas.create_line(p1_x, p1_y, p1_x, (p1_y-line_length), width=line_width, fill=p1_colour)
p1_y = p1_y - line_length
```

```
##### main:
window = Tk()
window.title("MyEtchASketch")
canvas = Canvas(bg=canvas_colour, height=canvas_height, width=canvas_width, highlightthickness=0)
canvas.pack()


window.mainloop()
```

Analysis of Code Box 5.2

First, it must be noted that p1 stands for player 1. The reason for having a player 1 is that you never know what is going to happen when you start out making a game. Ideas crop up and suddenly you want another player. OK, probably not for a MyEtchASketch game.

The variables

Instead of adding lots of squares to make our lines, the code is simpler if you draw lots of little lines. You make a square by setting the `line_width` equal to the `line_length`. This works well because a line has a beginning and end coordinate, which is just what we want to keep track of. The variables are listed in Table 5.1.

Code	What it means	Initial settings
`p1_x`	stores the *x* position of the end of the line	half the width of the canvas
`p1_y`	stores the *y* position of the end of the line	the height of the canvas
`p1_colour`	stores the colour of the line	`"green"`
`line_width`	stores the line width	5 pixels
`line_length`	stores the line length	5 pixels

Table 5.1 Variables for MyEtchASketch game.

The p1_move_N() function

`p1_move_N(event)` is going to be a function that sends the line drawn by player 1 up the screen.

event

The `event` argument contains information being passed to the function about which key was pressed. If we did not include event as an argument, we would get an error complaining that we passed 1 argument to `p1__move_N()` when 0 were expected.

global

At the start of our script, we declared all our variables and gave them some **default** values. As they are outside any functions, they are **global variables**. This means that they are available throughout the program. However, any variables declared inside a function are called **local variables**, which means that they are not available outside their function and will be lost when the function call is over. As we want all our functions to use our global variables we have to tell the function this, by re-declaring them inside the function, using the keyword `global`. This is only required if the function is going to change the variable. By doing this the function is using the same variables as the rest of the program.

The create_line() method

We are using the `create_line()` method from tkinter's canvas class:

```
canvas.create_line(arguments go here)
```

The arguments required are shown in Table 5.2 on the next page.

Arguments required by tkinter	Your supplied variables
`x1` (*x*-coordinate of beginning of line)	`p1_x` (current *x*-coordinate of player 1)
`y1` (*y*-coordinate of beginning of line)	`p1_y` (current *y*-coordinate of player 1)
`x2` (*x*-coordinate of end of line)	`p1_x` (current *x*-coordinate of player 1)
`y2` (*y*-coordinate of end of line)	`p1_y - line_length` (current *y*-coordinate of player 1 minus the length of the line)

Table 5.2 Arguments required for MyEtchASketch to move north.

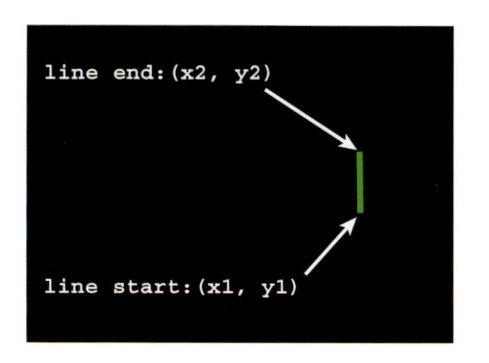

To draw on the canvas we create lots of little lines that always start with the same coordinates that the last one ended with. This is easier than making little squares. Instead, we draw green lines that are 5 pixels wide to match our line length. Thus, we need to supply two more optional arguments to the `create_line()` method as shown in Table 5.3.

Optional arguments	Your supplied variables
`width`	`line_width`
`fill`	`p1_colour`

Table 5.3 Optional arguments for MyEtchASketch.

As we are moving up the screen, it is only necessary to subtract the line length from `p1_y` but you must add one more line of code to this function to store the new `p1_y` position for next time.

Adding keyboard control

We simply use the `bind()` method from the `tkinter` window class and it just takes two arguments.

```
window.bind("the key board key name", our_function)
```

If we wanted the *a* key we would supply the argument `"a"` but for the *up arrow* key we give `"<Up>"`.

```
window.bind("<Up>", p1_move_N)
```

Adding keyboard control is actually very easy!

Yeah, I've heard that before.

Now add the code from Code Box 5.3 to your `myEtchASketch.py` file. When you run this, if all is well, you will find that by pressing the *up arrow* on your keyboard you can make a series of green squares 5 pixels wide by 5 pixels long.

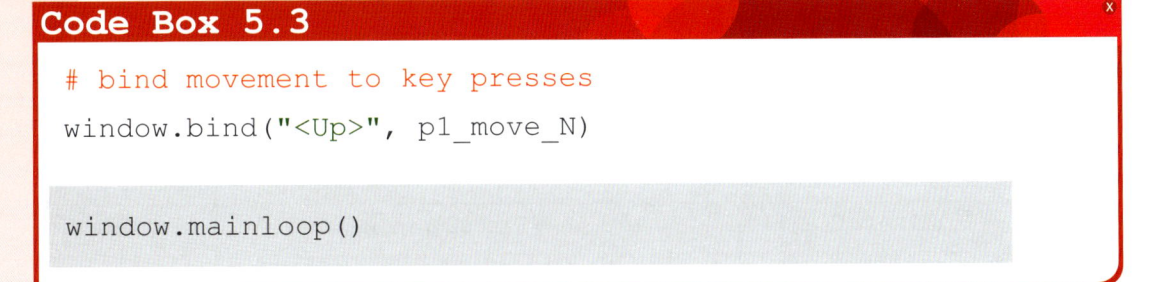

Code Box 5.3   x

```
# bind movement to key presses
window.bind("<Up>", p1_move_N)


window.mainloop()
```

See, it really was easy!

OK – it was easy!

Finishing off

Once you have movement upwards, you will find the other directions are easy to write code for. To move down we add 5 pixels to our *y*-coordinate, to move right we add 5 pixels to our *x*-coordinate and to go left we take 5 pixels from our *x*-coordinate.

Add the rest of the functions from Code Box 5.4 (this is the final step). Since we are repeating this code so often, this should indicate that there is probably a better way of writing this program. We will examine this in the activity section at the end of the chapter.

If you find your program does not run the first time; try to sort out any problems yourself. If you do get stuck though, you can download the code from the companion website.

copy...paste...copy...paste...copy...paste...there has to be a better way!

```python
# player controls
def p1_move_N(event):
    global p1_y
    canvas.create_line(p1_x, p1_y, p1_x, (p1_y-line_length), width=line_width, fill=p1_colour)
    p1_y = p1_y - line_length


def p1_move_S(event):
    global p1_y
    canvas.create_line(p1_x, p1_y, p1_x, p1_y+line_length, width=line_width, fill=p1_colour)
    p1_y = p1_y + line_length
def p1_move_E(event):
    global p1_x
    canvas.create_line(p1_x, p1_y, p1_x + line_length, p1_y, width=line_width, fill=p1_colour)
    p1_x = p1_x + line_length
def p1_move_W(event):
    global p1_x
    canvas.create_line(p1_x, p1_y, p1_x - line_length, p1_y, width=line_width, fill=p1_colour)
    p1_x = p1_x - line_length
```

```python
def erase_all(event):
    canvas.delete(ALL)

##### main:
window = Tk()
window.title("MyEtchASketch")
canvas = Canvas(bg=canvas_colour, height=canvas_height, width=canvas_width, highlightthickness=0)
canvas.pack()
# bind movement to key presses
window.bind("<Up>", p1_move_N)

window.bind("<Down>", p1_move_S)
window.bind("<Left>", p1_move_W)
window.bind("<Right>", p1_move_E)
window.bind("u", erase_all)

window.mainloop()
```

Chapter summary

In this chapter you have learned:

- how to use the tkinter library
- how to make your own MyEtchASketch game
- how to put an application in its own window
- how to attach functions to keyboard presses
- that 'copy and pasting' hints at a better way of doing things
- how to clear a canvas. (If you typed out the code you should have spotted an extra function that was sneaked in: `erase_all`(event) . This clears the screen when the user presses the **u** key on their keyboard.)

This chapter provides us with many possibilities for ideas. As you have organised your code well, the following Quick Ideas can be easily achieved by simply adjusting the variables at the beginning of your file.

I hope you have enjoyed learning to write code. You should be able to have a lot of fun with your new knowledge.

Quick Ideas

- Make `line_length` longer and see what happens.

- Change the colour a few times and find out what named colours tkinter supports.

- Generally change the square size to find a size that you like.

- Completely customise the code adjusting all the variables until you are happy.

Puzzle

Remember we said that copying and pasting indicates that there are better ways of coding. This puzzle encourages you to write better code.

Make a new function called `p1_move(x, y)` so that the four movement methods can be simplified to something like this.

```python
def p1_move_N(event):
    p1_move(0, -line_length)
```

There are several ways to do this. An example answer can be found on the website.

Also on the website you will find the code for a two-player game called `ourEtchASketch.py`. If you are feeling keen, you could try to make it yourself – it is not really very difficult and takes advantage of the better code structure from this chapter's puzzle. This two-player game is also fun for one player because it allows you to draw in two colours. It also provides the opportunity to give you a few more extra ideas.

Extra ideas

- Download `ourEtchASketch.py` and try drawing something colourful.

- Look at the code and see how easy it was to make this into a two-player game.

- Try it out with a friend as a cooperative drawing game.

- Try playing it as a timed competition to see who has the most squares visible at the end. The object is to draw over your opponent as much as possible. (**Hint:** It might be best to make the squares bigger.)

- Try playing a weird game of Tron. As there is no collision detection, you will have to be honest about when you collide. (**Hint:** If you do not know what Tron is, ask an adult.)

- Try making the canvas tall and thin and then having a race with a friend to the top of the screen.

- Make the racing game more interesting by putting some obstacles in the way. (**Hint:** draw some random-sized and coloured lines on the screen at the start just before the code that binds the functions to the keyboard.)

- Make up some other games of your own.

OK, serious fun!

Taking things further

When you have finished this book we hope you will want to continue to learn to code. Here are some other places and resources that you might wish to look at.

More Python

Other books in the series, found at this book's companion website: http://www.codingclub.co.uk

The official python documentation: http://docs.python.org/py3k/

PyGame Website: This site provides a set of modules that need to be downloaded that aid with making games. It has a community of Python coding enthusiasts and enables you to post your games for others to play.

Thinking like a programmer

http://armorgames.com/play/6061/light-bot-20
http://www.robozzle.com/

Other programming languages

The Scratch official website: http://scratch.mit.edu/
Java Programming: http://www.greenfoot.org/

Appendix

Some key bits of information

Companion website

Website: http://www.codingclub.co.uk

Here you will find answers to the challenges and puzzles at the end of chapters. The complete source code for all the projects is also here.

Escape sequences

Escape sequence	What they do
\n	creates a line return in a string
\t	creates a tab style indent in a string
\\	allows a backslash to appear in a string
\"	allows a speech mark to be used in a string

Table A1 Escape sequences.

Mathematical operators

Operator	Name	Example	Answer
*	multiply	2*3	6
/	divide (normal)	20/8	2.5
//	divide (integer)	20//8	2
%	modulus	20%8	4
+	add	2+3	5
–	minus	7–3	4

Table A2 Mathematical operators.

Comparison operators

Operator	Meaning
==	equal to
!=	not equal to
>	greater than
<	less than
>=	greater than or equal to
<=	less than or equal to

Table A3 Comparison operators.

End game code snippet

```
input("\n\nPress the RETURN key to finish.")
```

Basic tkinter code for activating a function via a key press

```
window.bind("<Up>", my_function)
```
or
```
window.bind("a", my_function)
```

Basic tkinter code for making a canvas to draw in its own window

```
from tkinter import *

##### Set variables:
canvas_height = 400
canvas_width = 600

##### main:
window = Tk()
window.title("My Game Title")
canvas = Canvas(bg = "black", height = canvas_height, width = canvas_width, highlightthickness = 0)
canvas.pack()
window.mainloop()
```

Use the random module to pick a number between 1 and 6

```
import random
dice_number = random.randint(1,6)
```

Glossary and index

argument   a piece of information that is required by a function so that it can perform
its task; usually a string or number, `my_function(arguments go here)`   36

'Bold' is not a special computer word. Mr Campbell said it would not be in the glossary.

bug   a piece of code that is causing a program to fail to run properly or at all   14

casting   the process of converting one data-type into another; e.g. sometimes a
number may stored as text but need to be converted in to an integer – this
can be done like this: `int("3")`   52

commenting   some text in a computer program that is for the human reader and is
ignored by the computer when running the program – in Python all
comments begin with a hash symbol `#`   30

comparative operator   sometimes called logic operators, they allow us to compare data in a
program; they include == and > (others are found in Table 3 in the Appendix)   25

data-type   different types of information stored by the computer, for example floats,
integers and strings   52

default   a value given to an argument or variable as a starting point   63

The Quick Quiz answers

Quick Quiz 1

Answer = 2

Quick Quiz 2

Answer = 11 divided by 4 also equals: 2 remainder 3

Quick Quiz 3

Answer = 1

Acknowledgements

Although this is a small book it has been a lot more work than I expected. My aim has always been to produce a series of books that are produced to a standard that young people deserve. To that end I sought an established publisher and my thanks have to go to Claudia Bickford-Smith for her enthusiasm for the project. I am so glad that Cambridge University Press were able to take me on. The hard work of Heather Mahy and Carl Saxton who had the unenviable job of keeping me on the straight and narrow while making the project a reality is also much appreciated.

A book that purports to teach coding to youngsters has to be tried out on youngsters. My thanks therefore must go to The Coding Club boys of Ewell Castle School and my youngest son Daniel who endured the early versions and helped me find out what worked and what (unfortunately for them) didn't.

It was fantastic when I realised that the Raspberry Pi foundation had the same aims and root motivations as myself and the encouragement of Jack Lang and the enormous help from Alex Bradbury in ensuring my code and Computer Science was technically correct was invaluable.

I also want to personally thank Ohio Art Company who own and sell the amazing Etch A Sketch® toy who were also very enthusiastic and quick to give me permission to use their registered trademarks.

Fran, I love the illustrations.

My two eldest sons have left the nest but thanks to modern technology have also shared the journey and made invaluable contributions and suggestions. Finally, writing books and programs in the evenings and holidays takes time. My eternal thanks go to my wife Rita for never begrudging me this time or complaining, even when listening to me talking about code snippets!

Thanks guys … thighs.

The author and publisher acknowledge the following sources of copyright material and are grateful for the permissions granted. While every effort has been made, it has not always been possible to identify the sources of all the material used, or to trace all copyright holders. If any omissions are brought to our notice, we will be happy to include the appropriate acknowledgements on reprinting.

p. 28 ImageZoo/Alamy; p. 36 Sukhonosova Anastasia/Shutterstock; p. 37 Stock Illustrations Ltd/Alamy; p. 55 Judith Collins/Alamy

The word mark, logo, and configuration of the Etch A Sketch® product are registered trademarks of the Ohio Art Company.